INTRODUCTION

Have you ever had to make up your mind and make a quick snap decision, such as choosing between a beige or black jacket, veggies for tonight's supper or beverages (coffee or tea? White wine or soda?} Just as often, choosing a given product for its use, looks and price is frequently a no-brainer. For much of the time, you already have some idea and information, such as how much money you have and wish to spend.

 But there are other decisions to be made involve a little more time to think through carefully and finalize. Spending the amount of time to arrive at such a decision is crucial and a good investment of time, as it minimizes future regrets, especially ones like "Had I only known!"

By thinking about the consequences ahead of time, you may have the advantage of making an informed decision. You will likely gather information for evaluative purposes that can help more subtle options more obvious.

Knowing what questions that need to be answered before making a decision and answering them truthfully and completely will should boost your confidence that the decision you made was the right one. You will likely feel more confident! This book will include questions that should be asked and answered before making a decision. And totally eliminate the "Had I only known!' factor.

Chapter 1 – You can't predict the future, but you can make things go your way with a little thought

Okay, so you've come across a situation that involves your making a decision about something that doesn't happen very often. Maybe the situation is raher complex, such as relocating to another city or town in order to keep your job. Or just quit and save yourself the hassle of selling your home and figuring out how and what to pack and a million other things.

But there's no reason to go into panic mode. It's just a matter of doing first things first. To begin with, do you like or are you unfamiliar with your new city or state? Have you visited it previously? What were your first impressions? Does the prospect of getting up in the morning and making a two-hour commute to your job in all types of weather faze you? Will your employer assist you in moving and getting situated?

Will you be offered other perks as well? How many and what are they? Your answers to these questions should indicate what the hassles will be and if enduring them will be worth your while and even increase your happiness and anticipation of the Big Move.

But the thing now is that you have to decide whether to relocate in order to keep your present job. Overall, how well does your job pay and what are your duties? How long have you been with your present employer? How have you been treated at work? Does your job seem secure or has there been rumors about lay-offs in the near future?

The Consequences of deciding NOT to relocate

. You'll be temporarily unemployed for possibly weeks or months before you land another similar job.

. You will be able to remain in familiar surroundings and among familiar people.

. You already know what is or isn't available in your area.

The Consequences of your Decision to Relocate

.You will have to become acclimate yourself to a different environment

. You will likely incur more expenses

. You may still have to resolve related issues with your partner

. You may change your mind

. You may quit your job

.Things may not work out as you have anticipated

Answering each question honestly will give you a few clues in handling a given situation and practically guarantee that you will be satisfied with the outcome. I mean really satisfied, having no regrets, sleepless nights, differences with your partner.

Working out the details on paper and/or discussion will help ensure a satisfactory outcome.

Chapter 3

Questions to consider before donating a car or other property to charity. When you first think about it, the idea of helping a given charity is a worthy idea. You're helping to support a cause that you truly believe in and help out folks with cancer, for example, or animals from being euthanized. In return, you may take a tax deduction for your noncash donation.

But whether to donate (and regret it later) or not is ultimately your choice. You have to think things through carefully before acting too quickly and wind up regretting your decision. Answering the

questions below may help the decision process run more smoothly---
and help you to avoid regretting your actions later.

.

. How well do you know the organization?

. How do you begin the process of making a donation?

. Once your car is taken away, the space in your driveway will be empty.

Your car will be gone for good. You will at first have to become used to

seeing an empty space.

. Why are you donating your car?

Why You May Still Have Doubts

because you don't want to think about paying for insurance,

registration, repairs, inspection, and so on? Is it also because you're

anticipating walking, bicycling, using public transportation in the future

and want more peace of mind?

. Is your car still reliable and drivable? Would you feel confident using it for driving long distances? Would you miss the freedom of being able to go whenever and wherever?

. Do you still like your car, in spite of its age and appearance? Does it still feature a smooth ride? Does it need any expensive repairs?

. Is the car the only vehicle you own? How long have you owned it? Does it give you any problems or not?

. Will you still miss it when it is no longer in its usual space?

> ➤ Your car will be sold sometime in the weeks ahead and you will be able to deduct that price from your taxes. The charity will supply you with a form to submit with your tax return, and the IRS will require you to complete Form 8283. The only issue here will involve having the charity complete certain sections and return that filled-out form back to you.

> ➤ You will have to wait, unless you can fax the form to the charity and have it returned to you almost right away. If you use snail mail, you should follow up, calling the charity to find out if they received the form and when you can expect them to return it to you.

➢ So you might want to consider if you can trust the charity to do that in a reasonable time. Otherwise, you run the risk of waiting until April 14, the day before the deadline for filing taxes!

➢ As you can see, a lot must happen before you donate a car or other property. Are you sure that you really want to go through the process and face the hassles? Think, and think again, especially if you really love your car. Once it has been sold, it is gone for good.

➢ A possible option is donating or even selling the car to a family member.

Chapter 4– Making Decisions on Your Home's Landscaping

You happen to like the landscaping surrounding your home. Maybe for years, you've found and used and trusted various landscapers to mow your lawn, trim the shrubbery and generally maintain or even improve the landscaping. But there is one landscaper whose professionalism has impressed you. This guy has been in business for awhile and is up to date on landscaping techniques and equipment. His fees tend to be fair.

But there comes a day when this guy will recommend that your front evergreen shrub should be pruned by telling you that the shrub obstructs the mailbox. That would be his only justification! If you press him with more questions on why, he won't likely have any but will insist on pruning the plant. At the same time, he'll simply reveal that after the pruning is done, you'll see wood, or bare branches. In the past, you've always rejected such proposals because your evergreen, though really old, still looked great in spite of its age and only seemed to need an occasional trim. But a pruning? That may be too drastic.

. If the plant will grow back, approximately when will that happen?

. Whyat will be the likely results of that pruning?

' Did your landscaper warn you, for example, that it would take a long time, possibly YEARS for the plant to grow back? Sometimes at least two or more years at least. In the meantime, your plant will look sparse and sick, with its original lush appearance destroyed. And as one expert stated, the plant will grow back, but it will never look the same. That is, you won't likely see a lush plant anymore, regardless of how often you feed and care for it.

. Before deciding if pruning is the right solution for your plant, try to imagine seeing bare branches for moths at a time and very few shoots on those branches. It will look terrible. It will become an eyesore very quickly. What other difference will pruning your evergreen shrub make?

Avoiding mistakes with young plants

I once received a young potted tomato plant. With good soiling, lots of warm sunshine and careful watering, the young plant thrived and produced numerous leaves. Eventually, it would have to be planted in the backyard. The question at that time was when.

So a week later, I tenderly lifted it from its pot and carefully planted it in a suuny area of my backyard. The young tomato plant looked so good!

But my lawn had to be cut and I placed small fat bricks around the plant before contacting my landscaper. Then I left the house to conduct some business. Later that afternoon, on my way home, I thought about the tomato plant and its supposedly secure place in my backyard. My worst fears were confirmed when I rushed home and saw the backyard. Sure, the grass was trimmed but my young plant was shorn of its leaves and nearly cut in half! I cried, then hurriedly tried to repair the damage. I visited a home goods store and stocked up on soil and tomato plant food. I also bought portable wooden fences to install around the plant. In spite of the effort, time and money spent, the young tomato plant did not survve its ordeal, Its stem turned a sickly yellow, its remaining leaves withered and died.

To help avoid these types of tragedies, consider

. which plants you prefer, vegetables, fruits or flowers.

. where in your yard would these plants survive and thrive?

.warning your landscaper of your plants' locations

' installing fences, not bricks on the perimeter of the area that the plants occupy.

Chapter 5-Discarding Old Clothing

You probably have at least one pair of jeans, tops and sneakers that you seem to wear most often. But what about the items that linger in or out ofyour closet? The items, for example that are casually draped over one or two chairs? The headboard of your bed? Or even on the floor?

With clothes all over the place, you have an untidy room or apartment and who needs that?

You've probably decided to discard at least some of that stuff, but how and when?

Questions to answer about stuff that you plan to discard

Begin with one of the items that you rarely wear:

. Does that article of clothing still fit and look good on you?

.How often do you wear it?

.What do you like about it? What, if any sentimental value does it have and why? What don't you like about it?

Did you buy that item? What did you pay for it?

Where do you usually store that item? Is it merely taking up space? Does its presence make your living space look untidy?

If you threw out that item today, would you miss it or not?

.

Chapter 6 – Thinking of Changing a Room's Décor? Deciding if the project "is a go" or not

You're tired of the way your bedroom/dining room/kitchen looks and can justify your concern/s. For example. There may be one or more cracks in the ceiling, the floor is worn, the room's painted ceiling and walls are faded or dirty and there is way too much clutter!

So what happens now?

Should you immediately plunge into the project, full speed ahead? Certainly not! The first question that you should ask yourself is what in that room would benefit most from change ie, something new. Is it its color, space (or lack of space)? How much would such a change cost to implement and can your budget accommodate it? If not, could you get a loan or perhaps borrow money? Would the cost create a lot of debt?

How much?

You'll also want to consider results of this change. Will the walls' new color clash with furniture and overall décor? For example, red and purple would definitely clash and give you headaches and make your eyes feel sore. You may be able to find viable solutions at a nearby store as Home Depot or Lowes. Sure, visiting and finding ways to get your project off to a perfect start will take time and even some money! But you should think of these as investments that will be worthwhile and producing desired results.

. While you're at it, consider what needs to be done BEFORE the room is painted or decorated. Will removing/discarding clutter take more time? And what about valuables as money or jewelry, which may need to be safely stored elsewhere, as in a safe? Will you need to buy a safe to accommodate your valuables? How much will that safe likely cost?

. Will you need new furniture too? What pieces would be needed and where would they be placed? How much would they cost altogether or separately? What store seems to carry furniture that you need or want?

You want to be happy with your investment without the rush or hassles. So take as much time as you need. After all, Rome wasn't built in a day as the saying goes. And its building, rest assured, took years!

Chapter 7 – Should You go Ahead and Buy That New Car?

Buying a new car! Sounds exciting and certainly something to look forward to. Like other important decisions that may have to make in your life, this decision merits time and effort. You want the best car you can buy and afford, You may have already decided that you needed a new car and that now is a good time as any.

First things first, however. You should have some idea of how frequently you'll use the car. Do you intend to commute to work every day or use it just to go out for recreational purposes? Will the car likely sit for long periods in your driveway and be used occasionally? Think again, as cars that sit in a spot for any length of time tend not to start easily when you turn the key in the ignition. My 1986 Toyota Corolla was like that because I tended to drive it infrequently. It was an excellent reliable car that remained problem-free for thirty years. And if I had to buy a new car, my choice would be obvious. It would be a

Toyota Corolla, hands down! I've also heard good things about the Prius. But you may be in the process of deciding.

So take the time you need and shop around for the make and model car that's right for you. Price various new cars. How much do they cost? Can you comfortably handle the car payments as well as other bills month after month?

. Think about the cars owned by family members and friends. Were those vehicles reliable? Had all kinds of mechanical problems? Were relatively easy to maintain? Did you like any of those cars and would consider newer models of those cars? Did you ask for recommendations and go online for further recommendations? What did you learn about the make and model that you're considering. If possible, get recommendations on various dealerships.

After some time, you've decided to buy a given vehicle. Congratulations!

You might begin dealerships recommended by family members and friends and even test drive potential new cars. Ask about financing your purchase. How much down and how much after that per month? What are the terms? How many payments are involved and when are they due? What are new features and can you opt to buy or decline buying? How much will it cost for car insurance and where can you get the best deal?

Go online and learn more about the car's make and model. Did you find glaring issues mentioned? Praise for the car in general from experts and buyers? Try joining a specific forum that focuses on the car that you are thinking of buying. Do plenty of comparison shopping too!

Finally, consider the color of your new car. What colors are available?

Are there plenty to choose? Remember that lighter colors as white or tan or silver,show dirt and other stains that may be easy or more difficult to remove. But they seem cooler in the summer heat too, On the other hand, colors as black or blue or maroon, though more conservative, may not require frequent washes. But dirt and droppings from nearby trees will eventually show and need to be removed.

. Cars nowadays also tend to have more gizmos and gadgets that are designed for additional comfort, convenience, and safety. How much time would you need to become comfortable with their features like airbags? During your test drive, have your dealer indicate the location and function of ndew features and discuss them a bit before you ultimately decide. Maybe even practice using them!

Time to decide! But there's no need to rush! Make sure that any doubts you may have or had are addressed. Get those burning questions answered once and for all. And happy motoring!

Chapter 8 Adopting a cat or dog

Cats and dogs make great pets and wonderful companions. And the sad part is that millions of unwanted cats and dogs wind up in shelters where they are eventually euthanized. This is also sad because they were innocent, loving sentient creatures. So by all means, find that perfect cat or dog for you at a shelter.

You may be surprised, though, to find that a few shelters don't euthanize their animals, though these places work hard to find homes for the animals. The staff that work in shelters are caring and compassionate about the animals they serve. In a few small shelters, though, you may be surprised to discover how knowledgeable staff members are. They seem to know a lot about specific dogs and cats and these animals' personalities! Once I saw a large calico cat who was very shy and remained sitting on her perch. I learned that the cat's name was Waffles. Waffles had been in the shelter for awhile, She had been briefly considered by potential adopters and passed over.

I was almost one of those potential adopters, but thought that Waffles seemed so sweet and looked so good that she was worth more consideration. I walked back to her cage. Waffles stepped off her perch and rubbed herself against the bars. I scratched her ear and heard her purr. Then a staff member appeared and told me that Waffles had never done that before for anyone! I knew that I was going to bring Waffles home with me. She'd be a great companion for me and my other cat, Leo, a Maxine Coon. Once in the house, Waffles ran in my bedroom and hid in the closet for two days. Then one quiet afternoon, she ventured out and began wandering around. I remained quiet, as I did not want to startle her or see her run back in the closet. Gradually, Waffles adapted and after a week, found her favorite places to sit and sleep. She enjoyed food and all kinds of treats. She became a sweet loving companion over time. And she was adopted from a shelter!

As you make plans to visit a shelter and adopt, you will not likely regret giving a shelter pet a forever home!

Visiting a Shelter

Besides hearing dogs barking and seeing other potential adopters peering at the pets up for adoption, you will quickly notice that each animal has been assigned a name! If you adopt a cat or dog whose name doesn't appeal, you can easily assign a name that you prefer and your pet will, over a short time, recognize that name.

You'll also notice a variety of temperaments among cats and dogs. Some of them are lively while others are more laid-back, either sleeping or relaxing in their cage. Should you wish to hold and pet a certain cat or dog, ask a staff member to take the animal out of its cage and escort you to a separate smaller room for being with a potential pet. Having more privscy to pet an animal you are considering for adoption allows that animal a little freedom and you some time to make up your mind.

Adopting my cat Julius was an easy process for me, as Julius, a male brown tabby, sat on my lap for a few seconds before jumping on a nearby shelf. I decided to adopt him in a few minutes. Julius remained calm during the ride home and in the house, preferred to explore before settling down on a radiator. Unlike Waffles, he didn't hide in a closet, but allowed himself to be petted and fed. To this day, Julius is well-behaved and sweet. He's bonded with my other cat, Priscilla, well, though he occasionally annoys her.

So is it a good idea to adopt a pet immediately or allow yourself to think about adopting?

It all depends. If your potential pet is rambunctious, you may need a little more time to pet-proof your home and buy supplies as food, a water dish and treats. If you're adopting a cat, you'll want to buy a litterbox. Consider whether regular cat litter will suffice or whether old newspapers will be better. With litter, you'll constantly be sweeping or vaccuming it off the floor. But you'll be able to scoop the waste easily and throw it in the garbage. Newspapers are another story and can be problematic to dispose of and replace. If your cat is anything like my Julius, he or she will likely mess them up, making it more difficult to remove and replace. Both methods have advantages and disadvantages, so pick yours.

Another thing about cats and even dogs is that usually, the animal chooses a place where it would feel comfortable sitting or sleeping, and it's not always where you think!

That place may require a soft cushion or towel or blanket or even a pet bed! Let your pet choose and take your cues from that.

In the weeks ahead, you'll find that your new pet has adjusted well to its surroundings with no problem! You've wisely kept it indoors, if it is a cat and you'll have it longer. Keeping a pet cat indoors protects it from dangers as being hit by a car and being injured by another cat, dog, or possum! And having adopted and saved one animal's life, you may feel inspired to adopt another to serve as a companion or playmate. After all, two may be better than one! Here's to enjoyable days ahead with your new pet!

Other Issues Involving Pets

; Food – There's supermarket cat and dog food and plenty to choose from and then there are "name" brands as Friskies and Temptations, which are noticeably more expensive! So which one is better for your cat or dog?

Buying the supermarket brand will save you some money, but you want a better quality of food for your pet's health and well-being. So you might want to opt for "name" brands. Or if you're really ambitious, consider cooking meals and treats for your pet. But be careful! While home-cooked food is certainly tastier and more wholesome, it will lack some necessary ingredients as taurine that are typically found in commercial pet food. To overcome that issue, do buy and serve commercial food, but vary that food with home-cooked and even baby food as chicken broth,carrots and corn.

Read the label on a jar of baby food and you'll quickly notice that no chemicals or preservatives have been added. Your pet may enjoy lapping up baby food and may avoid illnesses as kidney disease and stomach issues.

Also baby food is a little more expensive than canned pet food or just as expensive. Varying your pet's diet with natural foods will definitely avoid expensive visits to the vet and expensive foods recommended by your vet. Whatever you decide, opt for natural over processed food.

Affording Your Pet Unless your pet is a special breed, you shouldn't have to worry about grooming or other issues. And unless your pet has a pre-existing condition, it should require extra visits to the vet. Issues as fea and tick control may cost extra money, but that money is well-spent. Fleas multiply fast and can literally eat their host alive. If your house is infested with fleas, you may have a hard time getting rid of them. You may have to consider hiring a bug exterminator, but know that it will be expensive.

Find a reputable exterminator before you need one. Investigate exterminators serving your area. Do they provide telephone numbers? Gurantees? Do they show up when they say they will? How much does a basic service, as getting rid of fleas cost per visit? Are any specials avaiaible on services? Have there been complaints about services or the cost of those services?

Owning a pet should not be a hassle or a negative experience. Like children, pets need love, attention and good care. Some care will involve extra time or money. You might consider setting up a budget funded with a little extra money for unexpected expenses. Then if and when the unexpected does happen, you will be able to deal with it with a minimum of stress. Overall, it feels good knowing that you've saved an animal's life.

Chapter 9 Finding extra money to fund a project or activity

1. Write down how much money you spend per day and on what
2. Take advantage of sales to buy things that you tend to need and use most often
3. Reduce spending gradually
4. Manage your time so that you can run more errands while you're out. There won't be any need for multiple trips or additional expenditures.

5. Take your daily expense, like coffee, and trim it gradually, say, to one cup per week. Multiply its cost by the number of days that you went without and you'll see that you saved money!

6. Try to resist "impulse" buying, which takes a chunk from your disposable income and gives you yet another item to store on a shelf or in a closet or in the corner of a room. When your home is cluttered. It gives you less incentive to clean and organize. In time, simplest items become lost or misplaced and require time to find. Consider throwing out items that you haven't usred for a long time or don't plan to use anytime soon.